ESSENTIAL ELEMENTS
FOR JAZZ ENSEMBLE

A COMPREHENSIVE METHOD FOR JAZZ STYLE AND IMPROVISATION

By MIKE STEINEL

WELCOME to the exciting world of jazz! This book will help you get started by introducing the important elements of jazz style and improvisation. You'll also learn basic jazz theory and some highlights of the history of jazz.

The exercises and compositions in this book can be played by a full jazz ensemble, or individually with the CD. Listening to good jazz players is an extremely important way to learn, and playing along with the CD is an excellent way to hear how jazz is played. The full band arrangements in this book include "sample" improvised solos for study and reference. And remember…have fun playing jazz!

ABOUT THE AUTHOR

Mike Steinel is an internationally recognized jazz artist and educator. He has recorded with the Frank Mantooth Orchestra and the Chicago Jazz Quintet, and performed with a wide variety of jazz greats including Clark Terry, Jerry Bergonzi, Bill Evans, and Don Ellis. Since 1987, he has been a member of the jazz faculty at the University of North Texas where he teaches jazz improvisation and jazz pedagogy. He is the author of *Building A Jazz Vocabulary* (a jazz text) and numerous compositions for jazz ensemble.

The University of North Texas pioneered jazz education when it instituted the first jazz degree program in 1947. Its flagship ensemble, the One O'clock Lab Band has toured four continents and has been the recipient of four Grammy nominations. Throughout its history, UNT has produced a host of fine jazz talent. Alumni of the program can be found in all facets of jazz and commercial music.

Managing Editor:
MICHAEL SWEENEY

ISBN 0-7935-9624-6

HAL•LEONARD®
CORPORATION
7777 W. BLUEMOUND RD. P.O. BOX 13819 MILWAUKEE, WI 53213

JAZZ IS...

- AMERICAN MUSIC that originated at the beginning of the 20th century
- A BLEND of many influences:
  - African melodies, rhythms, and instruments
  - European melodies, harmonies, and instruments
  - Early American musical styles such as Blues, Work Songs, Spirituals and Hymns, Ragtime, and Marches
  - More Recent Styles such as Rock, Afro-Cuban, and other Latin styles
- HIGHLY RHYTHMIC MUSIC, having historical connections with movement and dance
- MOSTLY IMPROVISED — jazz musicians don't rely completely on written parts

THE JAZZ ENSEMBLE

- CAN VARY IN SIZE

  From Small Combos – usually three to nine pieces with individual instruments

  To Large Ensembles – made up of "sections" (brass, reeds, rhythm, and strings)

- EVERY PART IS IMPORTANT

  Unlike Concert Bands and Orchestras which may have many players on a part,

  Jazz Ensembles usually have one player on each part.

- HAS A RICH TRADITION

  The original "jazz" bands were marching bands that played for social events.

  Throughout the 20th century the instrumentation of jazz bands grew:

  Jelly Roll Morton's Band in 1926 had 7 pieces

  Duke Ellington's Band in 1942 had 17 pieces

  Stan Kenton's Neophonic Orchestra in 1955 had 23 players

  The standard instrumentation of the jazz band today is:

  4 trumpets, 4 trombones, 5 saxes, piano, guitar, bass, and drums

Traditional Set-up

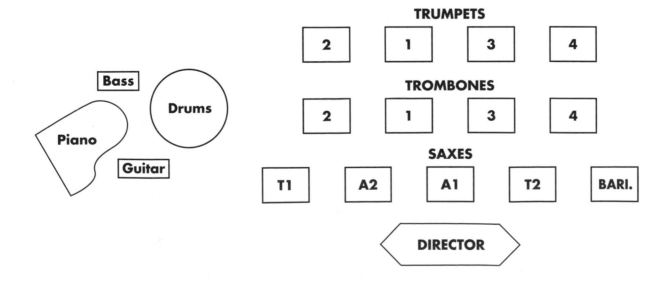

IMPROVISATION

- IMPROVISATION IS COMPOSING AND PERFORMING MUSIC AT THE SAME TIME
  - Jazz is usually improvised within the structure of a song or song-form
  - Music was improvised by the Greeks as early as 400 BC
  - Musicians of all cultures improvise to some degree

- IS JAZZ IMPROVISATION DIFFICULT?
  - Like learning a new language, it takes a little time but soon gets easier
  - The key: to start and not be afraid to make mistakes (a natural part of learning)
  - Everyone can learn to improvise with practice and help from a teacher

- HOW DO I START?
  - By listening to great jazz artists
  - By imitating the sounds you hear (and writing them down)
  - By developing good technique so you can play the sounds you hear in your head
  - By jumping in and giving it a try!

THE RHYTHM SECTION

All Jazz musicians need to understand the unique roles of the RHYTHM SECTION. Normally made up of piano, bass, guitar, and drums, it provides three of the basic elements of jazz performance:

- PULSE — steady time keeping
- HARMONY — playing the chords, providing harmonic accompaniment for melodies and improvisations
- RHYTHMIC INTERACTION — playing the rhythmic accompaniment for melodies and improvisations

Like a good conversation, jazz relies on interaction and communication.

All three elements are needed for jazz: Pulse, Harmony, and Rhythmic Interaction. But no one player in the rhythm section does all three jobs — they are divided among the players. If you map out the relationships, it would look like a triangle:

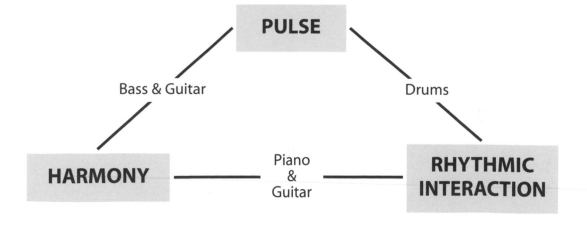

THE BASICS OF JAZZ STYLE

Attacks and Releases

In traditional music (Concert Band and Orchestra) you use a "Tah" articulation to begin a note and taper the note at the end.

In jazz it is common to use a "Doo" attack (soft and legato) to begin a note. It is also common to end the note with the tongue. This "tongue-stop" gives the music a rhythmic feeling.

1. ATTACKS AND RELEASES

Accenting "2 and 4"

For most traditional music the important beats in 4/4 time are 1 and 3. In jazz, however, the emphasis is usually on beats 2 and 4. Emphasizing "2 and 4" gives the music a jazz feeling.

2. ACCENTING 2 AND 4

Playing Doo and Bah (Full Value Notes)

In jazz, notes marked with a dash (tenuto) or an accent are played full value with a soft legato articulation. The scat (vocal) syllables "Doo" and "Bah" will help you hear the sound of these articulations. Remember in jazz it is important to play full value notes with a legato articulation.

Note: The "Bah" articulation is used only when vocalizing the scat syllables. "Bah" helps demonstrate the appropriate amount of accent. When articulating on your instrument use the syllable "Dah."

3. DOO AND BAH

Playing Dit and Dot (Short or Detached Notes)

In jazz, notes marked with a staccato or a roof top accent are about half of full value. The scat syllables "Dit" and "Dot" will help you hear the sound of these articulations.

4. DIT AND DOT

5. DOO, BAH, DIT, AND DOT

Swing 8th Notes Sound Different Than They Look

In swing, the 2nd 8th note of each beat is actually played like the last third of a triplet, and slightly accented. 8th notes in swing style are usually played legato.

5. SWING 8TH NOTES *Sing the scat syllables of each exercise before you play it.*

Tah Tah Tah Tah Tah   Tah Tah Tah Tah Tah   Doo Bah Doo Bah Dot   Doo Bah Doo Bah Dot

Quarter Notes

Quarter notes in swing style are usually played detached (staccato) with accents on beats 2 and 4.

Dit Dot Dit Dot

7. QUARTERS AND 8THS

Dit Dot Dit   Doo Bah Doo Bah Dot   Dit Dot Dit   Doo Bah Doo Bah Dot

8. MORE QUARTERS AND 8THS

Dit Dot Dit Dot   Doo Bah Doo Dot   Dit Dot   Doo Bah Doo Bah   Doo Bah Doo Dot

Important Tip: Notes at the ends of phrases are usually played short and accented.

Jazz Articulation Review

These are the four basic articulations in jazz and the related scat syllables for each.

Tenuto (full value)	Staccato (short, unaccented)	Long Accent (full value, accented)	Roof Top Accent (short, accented)
Doo	Dit	Bah	Dot

Quarter Notes

Quarter notes in swing style jazz are usually played staccato.

Staccato   *Legato*

Dit Dot Dit Dot   Doo Bah Doo Bah Doo Bah Doo Bah

Swing 8th Notes

8th notes in swing style jazz are usually played legato.

Syncopation in Jazz

When beats are played early (anticipated) or played late (delayed), the music becomes syncopated. Syncopation makes the music sound "jazzy."

14. SYNCOPATING BY ANTICIPATING THE BEAT (PLAYING EARLY)

15. SYNCOPATING BY DELAYING THE BEAT (PLAYING LATE)

16. WHEN THE SAINTS GO MARCHING IN – Without Syncopation

James Black and Katherine Purvis

17. WHEN THE SAINTS GO MARCHING IN – With Syncopation

18. RHYTHM STUDY FOR JA-DA

19. JA-DA – Full Band Arrangement – With Syncopation

Bob Carleton
Arr. by Mike Steinel

"Jazzin' Up" the Melody with Syncopation

Syncopation is the first step to improvising in a jazz style. Early jazz musicians syncopated all types of music, including marching band tunes, hymns, and blues songs. They called it raggin' the melody.

25. "JAZZIN' UP" A-TISKET A-TASKET

Original Melody

Jazzed Up (syncopated) Melody

Dit   Doo   Dit   Doo   Bah   Dit   Doo   Bah   Dot   Dit   Doo   Bah   Dit

Dit   Dot   Dit   Doo   Bah   Dot   Doo   Dit   Dot   Dit   Doo   Bah   Dot

"Jazzin' Up" the Melody by Adding Rhythms

Adding rhythms to a melody is another easy way to improvise in a jazz style. Start by filling out long notes with repeated 8th and quarter notes. Remember to swing the 8th notes (play legato and give the upbeats an accent).

26. "JAZZIN' UP" JINGLE BELLS

J. Pierpont

Original Melody

Jazzed Up Melody (rhythms added)

Doo   Bah   Doo   Bah   Doo   Bah   Doo   Bah   Doo   Bah   Doo   Bah   Dit   Doo   Bah

Doo   Bah   Doo   Bah   Dit   Dot   Doo   Bah   Dot   Dit   Doo   Bah   Doo   Bah   Doo   Bah   Dit   Doo   Bah

MAKE UP YOUR OWN (IMPROVISE)

27. LONDON BRIDGE   *Complete the melody in your own "jazzed up" way. Use only the notes shown in parentheses. Slashes on the staff indicate when to improvise.*

Original Melody

Jazzed Up Melody

Band   Solo   Band   Solo

Band   Solo – complete the melody

Helpful Hint: Using The Melody Is Never Wrong

When starting to improvise, keep the melody in your mind. It is a helpful guide for beginning improvisers.

Swingin' With Jack

28. RHYTHM WORKOUT · *Sometimes quarter notes are long.*

29. MELODY WORKOUT

30. SWINGIN' WITH JACK – Full Band Arrangement

Arr. by Mike Steine[...]

Style Review – Swing

- Use a soft "doo" attack rather than a "tah" attack
- Play quarter notes detached (staccato) unless otherwise marked
- Play notes followed by a rest staccato and accented
- Play 8th notes connected (legato) unless otherwise marked
- Play 8th notes with a triplet subdivision
- Accent 8th notes on the upbeats (the "and" of the beat)
- Accent quarter notes on beats "2" and "4"
- Use the scat syllables "doo", "bah", "dit", and "dot" to suggest the sound of each jazz articulation

Building Jazz Chords

Most jazz is harmonized with **Seventh Chords**. **Seventh Chords** are four-note chords built in thirds (every other note of a scale). A **Major Seventh Chord** uses the first, third, fifth, and seventh notes of a major scale.

Lowering the top note (called the seventh) of the **Major Seventh Chord** changes the chord to a **Dominant Seventh Chord**. Lowering the second (called the third) and top note (seventh) of a **Major Seventh Chord** changes the chord to a **Minor Seventh Chord**.

Chords have specific labels called **Chord Symbols**. The first letter in a **Chord Symbol** always indicates the root or the bottom note of the chord. The letters and numbers on the right indicate the chord type (major or dominant for example).

Chord Name	Chord Symbol
C Major Seventh	Cma7
C Dominant Seventh	C7
C Minor Seventh	Cmi7

33. MAJOR SEVENTH CHORD WORKOUT (Cma7)

(Play either note)

34. DOMINANT SEVENTH CHORD WORKOUT (C7)

(Play either note)

35. MINOR SEVENTH CHORD WORKOUT (Cmi7)

(Play either note)

The Dominant Seventh Chord is a "jazzy" chord

Because of its flattened seventh (often called a "blue note") the **Dominant Seventh Chord** has a very "jazzy" or "bluesy" sound.

The Blues Progression

The harmony of a jazz song is called the chord progression. The most common chord progression in jazz is the blues. Usually the blues is a twelve-bar repeated pattern using three **Dominant Seventh Chords**. The roots (bottom notes) of these three chords are usually the first, fourth, and fifth notes of the key of the blues.

36. LISTEN TO THE BLUES PROGRESSION – B♭ Concert

37. BLUES WORKOUT – Roots and Sevenths

38. BLUES WORKOUT – Roots, Thirds, and Sevenths

39. MAKE UP YOUR OWN – 2-Bar Solos using Roots, Thirds, and Sevenths

Building the Dominant Scale

You can build a "dominant scale" by inserting notes between the chord tones of the Dominant Seventh Chord. This scale "fits" (sounds like) the Dominant Chord.

40. BLUES WORKOUT – Dominant Scale

41. BLUES WORKOUT – Scale steps 1, 2, and 3

42. BLUES WORKOUT – Scale steps 1 through 5

43. BLUES WORKOUT – Scale steps 1 through 5, and ♭7

Helpful Hint: When you improvise, keep it simple. Don't try to play too many notes. Use occasional repeated notes and try to think of interesting rhythms.

44. MAKE UP YOUR OWN – 2-Bar Solos

PERFORMANCE SPOTLIGHT

45. OUR FIRST BLUES – Full Band Arrangement with Solos

Mike Steinel

14

St. Louis Blues (Composed by W.C. Handy)

46. RHYTHM WORKOUT

Doo Bah Doo Bah   Bah Doo Bah Dit Doo Bah   Doo Bah Doo Bah   Bah Doo Bah Dit Doo Bah

Doo Bah Doo Bah   Bah Doo Bah Dit Doo Bah

47. MELODY WORKOUT

W. C. Handy, often called "The Father Of The Blues," was a famous composer, bandleader, and music publisher. He was one of the first musicians to recognize the commercial potential of African/American folk music and he worked to incorporate these influences into the arrangements for his nine-piece orchestra.

Harmony Review

In Ex. 36 we learned about the blues progression in B♭ concert. Our version of St. Louis Blues uses a similar chord progression but in a different key: G (F concert).

48. LISTEN TO THE CHORDS FOR ST. LOUIS BLUES

I Chord   IV Chord   I Chord   V Chord   IV Chord   I Chord

49. BLUES WORKOUT FOR ST. LOUIS BLUES – Roots, Thirds, and Sevenths

50. BLUES WORKOUT FOR ST. LOUIS BLUES – Scale steps 1 through 5, and ♭7

Improvisation Review

On page 9 we learned how to improvise by using syncopation (jazzin' up the melody) and by adding rhythms. The melody to St. Louis Blues is already syncopated but we can add rhythms to make it "jazzier".

51. "JAZZIN' UP" ST. LOUIS BLUES – Adding Rhythms

52. ST. LOUIS BLUES – Add Your Own Rhythms

In the sections marked "Solo," take turns making up your own rhythms using only a single pitch (G).

Early Jazz

Jazz developed in the southern United States at the beginning of the 1900's. This new music, which wasn't even named "jazz" until 1917, borrowed elements from nearly all other styles of music: ragtime, European classical music, spirituals, hymns, work songs, field hollers, the blues, marching band music, and music from minstrel shows.

New Orleans was the center for jazz in the early years and New Orleans musicians such as Buddy Bolden, Joe "King" Oliver, Jelly Roll Morton, and Sidney Bechet were considered the finest performers of their time. "New Orleans Jazz" (or "Dixieland Jazz") focused on "group" improvisation with the trumpet, clarinetist, and trombonist often improvising at the same time over a steady accompaniment from a rhythm section made up of piano, banjo, drums, and occasionally bass.

After the first jazz recordings were made in 1917, the popularity of jazz grew rapidly. Jazz musicians traveled north to New York, Kansas City, and Chicago and then abroad. By the mid 1920's jazz was being performed throughout the world.

Louis Armstrong

Cornetist, Trumpeter, Vocalist

Louis "Satchmo" Armstrong (1900–1971) was born in New Orleans. Armstrong became famous playing with the bands of "King" Oliver and Fletcher Henderson before starting his own band in the mid 1920's. In addition to being a great trumpeter, he was a great singer as well and invented a style of singing using nonsense syllables which is known as "scat". He traveled the world many times in his long career and became the most famous jazz musician of his day.

Improvising on the Melody

Jazz musicians often improvise "on" or "around" the melody of a song. There are many ways to change a melody to create an improvisation.

53. ST. LOUIS BLUES – Original Melody

54. ST. LOUIS BLUES – Changing Rhythms

55. ST. LOUIS BLUES – Repeating Parts of the Melody

When there are pauses in the melody, repeat notes or groups of notes.

56. ST. LOUIS BLUES – Filling in the Skips

Skips in the melody can be filled in with the scale steps.

57. ST. LOUIS BLUES – Adding "Wrong" Notes (Chromatic Ornamentation)

A "wrong" or dissonant note (usually a half step off) can create a great jazz effect if it leads into a "good" melody note.

PERFORMANCE SPOTLIGHT

58. ST. LOUIS BLUES – Full Band Arrangement

W. C. Handy
Arr. by Mike Steinel

59. DEMONSTRATION SOLO FOR ST. LOUIS BLUES

18

Building the Blues Scale

The *Blues Scale* is a 6-note scale often used with the *Blues Progression*. Compare this scale with the major scale. The lowered (or flatted) notes are called "blue" notes and should be played with a bluesy feeling.

60.

61. THE BLUES SCALE – With the Blues Progression

62. BLUES WORKOUT – Blues Scale (1, ♭3, and 4)

63. BLUES WORKOUT – Blues Scale (1, ♭3, 4, and ♭5)

64. BLUES WORKOUT – Blues Scale (1, ♭3, 4, ♭5, 5, and ♭7)

65. MAKE UP YOUR OWN – 2-Bar Solos

Riffs and Licks

Riffs and licks are short melodies that jazz musicians use when improvising. Riffs and licks often are built using the notes of the blues scale. In solos and songs they are often repeated two or three times. It is important that beginning improvisers memorize common riffs and licks.

66. RHYTHM WORKOUT #1

67. RHYTHM WORKOUT #2

68. COMMON RIFFS – Using Notes of the Blues Scale

69. MORE COMMON RIFFS – Using Notes of the Blues Scale

70. THE MAJOR BLUES SCALE
This is another type of blues scale and is made up of the 1, 2, b3, 3, 5, and 6 of a major scale.

71. COMPARE THE BLUES SCALES

Jazz Expression – Bends and Scoops

72. THE BEND –
Start the note on pitch, lower it momentarily, then return to the original pitch. Bends can be executed with the embouchure or the fingers or a combination of both.

73. THE SCOOP –
Slide into the note from below pitch. Scoops can be executed with the embouchure or the fingers or a combination of both.

74. MAKING THE BLUES SCALES SOUND "BLUESY" –
To sound authentic, certain notes of the blues scales are usually "scooped" or "bent". Bending and scooping these "blue notes" gives these scales a sad emotional quality.

The minor blues scale has three blue notes.

The major blues scale has two blue notes.

75. COMMON RIFFS – Using Notes of the Major Blues Scale

76. MORE COMMON RIFFS – Using Notes of the Major Blues Scale

Improvising with Questions and Answers (Call and Response)

Playing jazz is like having a conversation. The riffs and licks of a blues song or improvisation often sound like questions and answers. Usually, the "Question Riff" is played twice followed by a contrasting "Answer Riff" which is played one time. This "Question and Answer" way of playing music is called "Call and Response".

77. QUESTIONS AND ANSWERS

79. MAKE UP YOUR OWN ANSWER WITH THE BLUES SCALE

80. MAKE UP YOUR OWN QUESTION WITH THE MAJOR BLUES SCALE

The Swing Era

In the 1930's and 40's, the orchestras of Duke Ellington, Count Basie, Benny Goodman, Glenn Miller, and Fletcher Henderson created a new type of dance music called swing. The strong beat and smooth "big band" sound made swing the most popular music of the time.

Edward Kennedy "Duke" Ellington (1899–1974) grew up in Washington, D.C. and led a band nearly all of his life. Although Duke was a gifted pianist, he is most remembered for his compositions and orchestrations. It is estimated that he wrote over one thousand works. Ellington is considered by many to be the most important jazz composer of the 20th century.

Duke Ellington

Count Basie

William "Count" Basie was born in Red Bank, New Jersey (1904), but his style of big band music is associated with Kansas City. In the early 1930's, Basie joined the Bennie Moten Orchestra, a "riff" styled band that specialized in playing the blues and performed primarily in the midwest. When Moten died in 1935 the "Count" took over the band, and under his leadership it became one of the most popular jazz bands of the era. Even after Basie's death in 1984, The Count Basie Orchestra continued to tour and please jazz audiences around the world.

PERFORMANCE SPOTLIGHT

81. **"RIFFIN' AROUND"** – **Full Band Arrangement**

Mike Steinel

82. DEMONSTRATION SOLO FOR "RIFFIN' AROUND"

Bebop

In the early 1940's, musicians began experimenting with a new kind of music which they called Bebop. Bebop was often much faster than swing music and its melodies and harmonies were much more complex. Swing bands played music primarily for dancing and focused on "ensemble" playing while the Bebop combos played for listening and emphasized improvisations.

83. RHYTHM WORKOUT

84. MELODY WORKOUT

Theory Review – The Dominant Scale (The Mixolydian Mode)

On page 12 we learned that the dominant scale can be built by inserting notes between the tones of a dominant chord. The dominant scale is also known as the mixolydian mode ("mode" is another name for "scale").

G Dominant Seventh Chord   *G Mixolydian Mode*

85. MIXOLYDIAN WORKOUT – Scale Steps 1–5

86. MIXOLYDIAN WORKOUT – Scale Steps 1–7

Bebop Uses "Wrong" Notes (Chromatic Ornamentation)

On page 16 you learned how you could improvise on a melody by adding "wrong notes" to the melody. You can also improvise on scales by adding "wrong" notes to the scales. Adding wrong notes is called chromatic ornamentation and bebop musicians in the forties made these "wrong notes" an important part of their improvised melodies.

87. "WRONG NOTES" CAN SOUND WRONG

88. "WRONG NOTES" CAN SOUND GOOD

Notes that don't belong to the sale can sound good if they lead into good notes (notes in the chord).

89. CHROMATIC WORKOUT – Filling in the Scale

Put the "good" notes on the downbeats and the wrong notes on the upbeats.

90. CHROMATIC WORKOUT – Filling in the Scale with Triplets

Put the "good" notes on the downbeats and the wrong notes on the upbeats.

91. CHROMATIC WORKOUT – Enclosing the Good Notes

Play 1/2 step above, then play 1/2 step below, then play the "good" note (a note from the chord).

The Bebop Lick

The Bebop lick starts on a scale tone, moves by half steps down a step, and then returns to the original note. It is a very common Bebop melodic device.

92. CHROMATIC WORKOUT – Using the Bebop Lick

Bebop Scale

On page 25 you learned how jazz musicians add "wrong notes" to scales. It is very common for improvisers to add a note between the seventh and root of the mixolydian mode to make a new scale called the **Bebop Scale**.

93. COMPARE THE MIXOLYDIAN MODE AND THE BEBOP SCALE

Bebop scales sound good with dominant chords because when they are played in 8th notes, the downbeats are always notes in the chord.

94. BEBOP SCALE WORKOUT – Running Down the Scale

95. BEBOP SCALE WORKOUT – Running Down from 3 to 7

96. BEBOP SCALE WORKOUT – Running Up from 5 and Ending on 7

97. BEBOP SCALE WORKOUT – Keeping the 8th Notes Going

98. TRADING OFF WITH THE BEBOP SCALE

Charlie Parker

Charles Christopher Parker (1920–1955) who was known to jazz fans as "Bird" grew up in Kansas City. As a young boy he idolized Count Basie's star tenor saxophonist, Lester Young. "Bird" became a virtuoso performer on alto sax whose solos displayed fire, brilliance, and a keen understanding of the blues. Although he died before he received the recognition he deserved, his style became widely studied and imitated.

Dizzy Gillespie

John Birks Gillespie (1917–1993) was born in South Carolina. While touring with the Teddy Hill Band, he earned the name "Dizzy" because of his clowning and horseplay. His main influence was Roy Eldridge who was perhaps the most brilliant trumpet soloist of the swing era. In addition to being a great trumpeter, "Dizzy" was an entertaining showman. His puffed cheeks and bent horn made him a recognizable figure the world over.

PERFORMANCE SPOTLIGHT

99. "BOPPIN' AROUND" – Full Band Arrangement

Mike Steinel

100. DEMONSTRATION SOLO FOR "BOPPIN' AROUND"

Latin and Rock Styles

Latin Jazz or Jazz Rock styles are played much differently than swing style. The 8th notes in Latin and Rock are played evenly, and articulations are often quite different than in swing style.

101. COMPARE THE 8TH NOTES

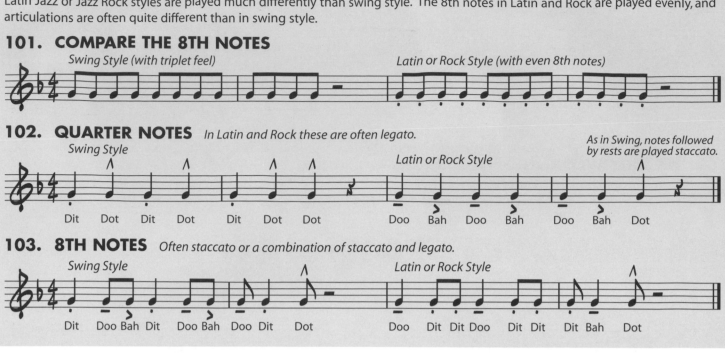

102. QUARTER NOTES *In Latin and Rock these are often legato.*

103. 8TH NOTES *Often staccato or a combination of staccato and legato.*

104. LATIN/ROCK RHYTHM WORKOUT #1

105. LATIN/ROCK RHYTHM WORKOUT #2

106. LATIN/ROCK RHYTHM WORKOUT #3

107. MAKE UP YOUR OWN

In the sections marked "Solo," take turns making up your own rhythms using only a single pitch (G).

Salsa Caliente

108. RHYTHM WORKOUT

Note: Sometimes in Latin jazz 8th notes are played legato or connected.

109. MELODY WORKOUT

Theory Review – The Minor Seventh Chord

On page 11 we learned that lowering the third and seventh of a Major Seventh Chord changes the chord to a Minor Seventh Chord.

110.

G Major Seventh Chord   G Minor Seventh Chord

1   3   5   7   5   3   1   1   ♭3   5   ♭7   5   ♭3   1

Building the Dorian Mode from the Minor Seventh Chord

Adding notes between the chord tones of the Minor Seventh Chord creates a new scale called the Dorian Mode.
The Dorian Mode "fits" or sounds like the Minor Seventh Chord.

G Minor Seventh Chord   G Dorian Mode

1   2   ♭3   4   5   6   ♭7   8

111. DORIAN MODE WORKOUT – Scale Steps 1–5

112. DORIAN MODE WORKOUT – Scale Steps 1–8

113. DORIAN MODE WORKOUT – Scale Steps 1–9

114. DORIAN MODE WORKOUT – Skipping notes and moving around

115. MAKE UP YOUR OWN – 2-Bar Solos Using the Dorian Mode

Blues Scale Review

The *Blues Scale* also sounds good with the Minor Seventh Chord and is common in Latin and Rock styles.

116. BLUES SCALE WORKOUT – 1, ♭3, 4, and ♭5

117. BLUES SCALE WORKOUT – 1, ♭3, 4, ♭5, 5, and ♭7

118. MAKE UP YOUR OWN – 2-Bar Solos Using the Blues Scale

Jazz Fusion

The term **Jazz Fusion** is used to describe a type of jazz that combines non-jazz styles with jazz. In the 1950's, jazz musicians began experimenting by borrowing rhythms, forms, and instruments from many other types of music. Since that time jazz has been fused (or combined) with classical music, latin music, rock music, and Indian music, to name a few. **Jazz Fusion** often features a rhythmic style that uses even eighth notes.

In addition to playing bebop and swing, **Miles Davis** (1926–1991) was a pioneer of "Jazz Fusion" styles. He was truly one of the most innovative jazz musicians of the 20th century.

Miles began his career with the great bebop saxophonist Charlie Parker but quickly emerged as a leader who became and remained a trend setter for the rest of his career. He had a particular gift for finding and nurturing the most talented young musicians of the day. The list of musicians who played in his bands is a veritable who's who of modern jazz and includes John Coltrane, Cannonball Adderley, Herbie Hancock, Chick Corea, Tony Williams, Bill Evans, and John McLaughlin.

Miles Davis

PERFORMANCE SPOTLIGHT

19. SALSA CALIENTE – Full Band Arrangement

For solos on this tune, use either the G Dorian Mode (shown) or the G Blues Scale. Both will sound good with Gmi7 and C7.
On the accompaniment CD the solo section is played a total of 6 times. In performance, the solo section may be repeated as many times as needed.

Mike Steinel

20. DEMONSTRATION SOLO FOR SALSA CALIENTE

121. Jazz Ornamentation and Expression

In order for music to sound jazzy, it must be played with appropriate jazz expression. There are many ornaments and articulations which are peculiar to jazz and necessary to achieve a characteristic jazz feeling. These are some of the most common ornaments:

Bend — Start the note on pitch, lower it momentarily, then return to original pitch.

Fall — At the end of the note let the pitch fall off. Falls may be executed with the emboucher or the fingers or a combination of both. Falls can be short or long.

Scoop — Slide into the note from below pitch. Scoops can be executed with the emboucher or the fingers or a combination of both.

Doit — Slide the pitch upwards at the end of the note.

Plop — Slide down to a note from above slightly before the note is to be played. Plops can be short or long.

Glissando — Slide from one note to the next smoothly. Glissandos may be executed with the emboucher or the fingers or a combination of both.

Flip — Often called a turn, the flip is executed by quickly playing a note above the original note (usually a step or half step), returning to the original note and then proceeding to the next written note.

Chord and Scale Review

Chord Type	Chord Symbol	Related Scale or Mode for Improvisation	
Major Seventh	$C_{MA}7$	C Major Scale	
Dominant Seventh	C^7	C Mixolydian Mode	Note: the Blues Scale can be used with Dominant Seventh Chords, Minor Seventh Chords, and the entire Blues Progression · C Blues Scale
Minor Seventh	$C_{MI}7$	C Dorian Mode	C Blues Scale